KUMINA QUEEN

for Ms. Katie, Ethel, Ignota and Ma Ma Minott

MONICA MINOTT

KUMINA QUEEN

POEMS

PEEPAL TREE

First published in Great Britain in 2016
Peepal Tree Press Ltd
17 King's Avenue
Leeds LS6 1QS
UK

ISBN 13: 9781845233174

Supported using public funding by
ARTS COUNCIL
ENGLAND

CONTENTS

Fisherman's Net	7
Penelope to Calypso	8
Columbus	9
Meeting a Fake West Indian at Yale	10
Dockside	12
Belly Pain	13
Crosses to Bear	14
Jemima's Wait	15
Choice	16
Journey to Paradise	17
River Mumma's Fate	18
Live & Direct	20
Good Hair	21
Cold Lemonade	22
Nostalgic December	23
Easter Sunday Morning	24
Sunday Verandah Story	25
Making Plans to Leave	26
Mama Said There Would Be Days Like This	27
Broken Bottles	28
Sweet Milk Creek	29
Travelling Under	31
Dance, Girl, Dance	32
Reader Woman	33
Sister Bernice	34
Shabba	35
Straw Flowers Growing in Miami Like Weed	37
Romping Shop	39
Fire Deh a Muss-Muss Tail	40
Navigating the Middle Passage	41
No Salt	42
On the Edge of the World	43
Stickfighters	44
Kumina Queen	45

Sold Again (Generations Now)   46
Silencing the Stones   47
Addiction   48
Gardener's Justice   49
Lychee Guard   50
Duppy Run   51
Blood Flowers   52
Point of View   53
Last Rites to Menses   54
Ric   55
Right to Die   56
Sign Birds   57
Dead Children are Dead   58
Direct Debit   59
Travel Advisory   60
White Roses   62
Bird Shooting Season   63
Drop-Pan Game   64
2008 News Report on Fidel   65
Casket Piece   66
Final Office   67

FISHERMAN'S NET

The dreadlocks from Little Bay
did not worry about worry.
Chilled by the sea breeze,
icy beer and a spliff,
I could tell, he was irie
as he turned to the music,
with the rhythm of the rising tide.
I selected a yellow-tail snapper
from his catch. "Come home
and cook for you," he smiled,
flashing a gold-capped tooth.
I laughed that throaty unnerving
laugh, but he never flinched.
Can't be sure of the sequence;
the music lapped us into
knee-high grass and the sea spray
settled like the skin around my nipples,
and thighs knotted like mangrove roots
giving in to the deep, held
by the strength of his arms
and the cry of the snapper,
caught.

PENELOPE TO CALYPSO

I is the girl who live up the rocks
beyond you, and yes, after twenty years
I still did tek him back; you only
know 'bout seven. So long he was
gone, I had to see the scar on his
thigh to know him. Buffeted
by sea savages, any man would be glad
to have someone bathe and 'noint him
with oils. So you play your part,
and as for the seven years, much respec'.
During that time I fell for
a beautiful able-body fisherman
from Little Bay – another
impossible situation.
Anyway, Odysseus is like driftwood;
long before he met you and me
he belong to the sea.
When driftwood wash up,
they make interesting furnishings
and conversation piece – if you into
that sort of thing. So when 'Dysseus
drop in and we walk the sands,
don't bear no grudge.

COLUMBUS

You were here
living
loving
and free
I happened
upon you
everything changed
and it seems right
to tell the world
I discovered you.

MEETING A FAKE WEST INDIAN AT YALE
(for Betty Neals)

"And where are you from?" Jill the traveller from Greece
asked the newcomer. "I live in Brooklyn, but I am
really from the islands."

I looked up, having established my presence
as the one quintessential island girl.
For two days there was Caribbean unity.

And here she come, trying to shift my sunshine. Cho!

So many abandoned the Petit Piton of St Lucia,
the slippery slopes of Dunns River Falls in Jamaica,
the clang of pan in Trinidad; each an excuse to come home.

Yes, they wait till sunset suit them out.
If they do come, they cold as stone, light as ashes
with no shiver, no reggae left in their bones.

I let Betty talk her talk, I know her type.

They take Jesus off the cross when it suit them,
seh they are West Indians through and through.
After quoting scripture, they sing the verse out of tune.

I asked Betty, "So when last you visit, chile?" It was then
she confessed, "Is one time I ever visit the islands, only
after Papa died. I went to find family, those he left behind,

for that is how Papa put it, before he shut his eyes."
Now you see my trial, though I want vex with Betty,
I can't; she trying to find a place to warm a frostbitten heart.

So I small up myself, and share the space,
especially after Betty said, "Is like a island spirit tek me."
And *spirit tek* is one sure test to know if you belong.

DOCKSIDE

Great grandmother on my mother's side had plenty Carib in her blood.
Hair thick and long to her waist, she could ride horse, kill chicken
and gut fish better than any man. Catherine Henry, called Katie,
knew how to set her trap, how to row her canoe to the cays.
Real fishermen found her amusing, till they saw her catch
as she headed back to Oracabessa, a quirky smile on her face.
Katie could sew any new style that took her fancy;
Busha bared himself, said, "Ketch me."
So she stitched her heart into Busha's inners.
After a few years together, rowing and stitching,
Busha became like the sea and this knock-down-
gorgeous hot-steppa became just Mama.
Nothing prepared her for his announcement,
"Wife and two children coming." The blood
of every Carib travelling like an arrow
en route to a slaughtering cloaked her.
Katie fainted. It took some time to
shed her rage, be rid of a blistered,
waterlogged Busha's ghost.

Like her grandmother, mother's wounded hands
would always say "yes". She was nurse, scribe,
builder, lawyer, teacher, friend. Knowing the time
when slave women were not allowed to read,
Katie taught Mama and the other grandchildren.
And, like construction workers, with sleeves
rolled up, we now search words for meaning.
We dissect sentences to identify hope; we argue
each case for Katie, Ethel, and Mama. We row
with Katie back to the cays, hoping
to catch her line of vision.

BELLY PAIN

When I tell the man I pregnant, he cough.
He know to give woman belly and grief, but
when time come to rally round: dry cough.
For the remaining six months, he missing.

Mama wash her hands of me, clean, clean;
seh she bring me up in church, and this is how
I repay her, bring shame down on the family,
seventeen, no man, and carrying belly.

But the sex was sweet. He offered me a ride
from school gate, man with pretty car.
The third day he took me home, I imagined
I was his girlfriend, his hands all over me.

But after the coughing and hissing,
I sat up and looked around: woman picture
on the dresser, children shoes in the hallway,
and me, walking in no man's land, parched dry.

Between that day and the pain, it was
me and me alone pissing, till Mama relent.
She hold me close and said, "Chile you must
bear upon misfortune, save you eye water.

Is the road you choose you walking on;
many a woman walk there before; every
loss is gain, till the pain, till the pain come,
only then you must bear down."

CROSSES TO BEAR

The best thing Len ever did
was leave. Never mind
the six children – they'll grow.
I understand how a chocolate-
brown, six-foot tall, hazel-eyed, athletic-
build man got you, but Lord knows
a man needs to be good
for something other than that.

Still, when sea breeze carries
the smell of jasmine, you remember
Mama's sad eyes when he called,
the evening walks up the steep
hillside in Port Maria where
knees buckled and the salt spray
lingered on your eyelashes.
You thought that was love.
How he held you tight
never prepared you.

Some say the cross saved you –
persistent screams for Jesus.
A witnessing voice over
the din and dizzy of distress
brought an end to your slide.
A fighting self expelled all
feelings of suicide.
Now you live in persistent praise.
Some say Mama and her Jesus
came… jasmining the air.

JEMIMA'S WAIT
(*for Derefe*)

Mama Jemima was always looking out,
pedalling her sewing machine,
stitching our lives back together.
Every time breeze blow the curtain
and the dogs barked, she jumped to her feet –
"Jimmy come, Jimmy come!"
– her heart racing to meet him,
tripping over her basket, scattering
thimble, scissors and pins.
It was my job to gather those pins
and pray with Mama. Her faith was strong,
even after thirteen years.
Before she opened the front door, she said,
"Thank you Jesus, thank you Lord."
But Daddy remained a no-show.
Mama would return to her sewing,
the weight of her heart pedalling,
the old machine listening.
"You got a six-month-stay; you leave me
with two children; Johnny just cutting teeth;
now he is a teenager; perhaps you dead,
for you could not be so forgetful.
And Peaches, she don't know who to trust.
I am still the wife of your youth
but you put me down like figurine
to gather dust. Today I set down the date:
20th August 2012; today I will forget you."
But soon the gate rattled. Mama
jumped to her feet: "Jimmy come!
Jimmy come! Jimmy come!"

CHOICE

Granny said, "When you enter a forest and it gets dark,
is not a good omen. You carrying a spirit wanting
to return to the core of the earth." But we
grew up in a time of throw away and forget,
so Granny's message never bother us.
We treated her sayings like rusty nails,
sharp and toxic, to be avoided.

After we turn thirteen, she preached:
"Many that enter the forest full, come out empty.
Better keep that secret pass shut. Wolf moon
tear flesh and leave the bones unburied."
Is only now I understand that sermon.
Only now I see your tiny hands and feet,
your heartbeat steady. Just a procedure,
they said. "Woman has rights over her own body."
But what were your rights when the suction ripped
you away from the safe warm inside, pulled you
into a cold sterile chamber before spewing you out
into a drain that led to a pit?

Granny said she couldn't worship
because of me. The forest has overtaken
our garden, bones scattered, eyes dark,
the glinting edge of the blade below dead leaves.

JOURNEY TO PARADISE

Imagine her too tired for conversation
after a long day at the office.
Imagine her stumbling up a flight of stairs
drunk from imbibing the rage
of dissatisfied taxpayers, walling
her into a cubicle, shutting off
the air of reason. She is spent.
Imagine him waiting to greet her,
share with her, passion boiling over
on a stove red-hot from wait.

Imagine if we could imagine today
thirty years ago, who we would
become. Imagine me stepping
out of the car after the first kiss,
me, pulling my skirt down as
tricky fingers inched up in a
quest to find luck. So quiet
now, even a humming bird would be
afraid to hum in paradise.

RIVER MUMMA'S FATE
(For Lorna G – The River Wanted Out)

Ah child, is because you don't know seh
is drop, I drop off the edge of the world,
so come I reach river bottom.

Is like I was hiding in the river over three-hundred years,
leaving a few uncared-for urchins to fend
for themselves, while I lap my tail, grow scale

and get broad, till they call me River Mumma.
I remember singing Sankey and dancing Kumina,
Mento and Fallback. One of them tek me over the edge.

I remember planting yam and coco
that feed the whole village. Many times I hear
singing echoing in the deep, and I want to join them.

But what you don't know, you don't know.
Is my tears start the river! All the time me find
rock bottom, is tears that save me. Sun fish and shark

know the story of deep down. They recognize a fellow
traveller. Now and then salmon invite me to take a run,
and when they jumping into the sunlight, nothing prettier.

I know time coming to leave river bottom, shed my scales.
Living in the water wasn't too bad. I made friends with
oyster, not to mention shark and janga; my gold

teeth, comb and pearl necklace is solid proof. But
there is something called time; it carry you like the sea,
you can't escape it. There is a time when river come down,

and a time for dry river. Sometimes river run straight,
sometimes it divide. Every woman have that natural divide,
is just who we willing to show. The gold comb and pearls was

never mine; I can leave those behind. What bothering me
is mi don't quite remember the reason for so much tears,
why river come down and turn sea.

LIVE & DIRECT

Ignota Elouise sits in her easy chair –
not a place she had relished
in her youth,
her line of vision halted
by grilles and doors,
her movements restricted,
but her voice still strong.
"Stefanie, girl, the Prime Minister
holding Live & Direct meeting
in Meadowbrook School hall tonight,
but your mother, she
not interested in those things.
When I was Elouise
I'd have been there.
There are questions
to be answered: the roads…
but I am not going anywhere
much these days;
age keep me inside,
but a hear seh
everybody turn shut-in
after dark; things never worse.
Factories closing.
All we hear is lay-off,
lay-off and downsizing.
When I was Elouise
he would have to answer,
but the meeting going on now, chile,
and all I can do is wait
to hear the news.

GOOD HAIR

I grew up an only child with mother
and her four sisters. Aunt Jackie, I remember
best for her hair combing. There was no
saying no to her. If one fidgeted,
she'd brush every strand until it was in place,
sweep my hair back, reining in the offenders.
The conk was reserved for serious
offences, like not paying attention to her stories.

She'd appear once a week and insist
my hair needed untangling.
"So you turning dread?" she'd say.
"Look how God give you hair like Aunt Katie
and you playing fool with it. You hair is you beauty!
Katie pretty so till, and her hair hold any man
except Busha." Nothing prepared her for his
announcement, wife and two daughters coming.
Katie was never herself again.

Next came the pinning of the bun.
It was then she'd retell the story of Grandfather
who went to war and was lost at sea. I dared not move.

But none of these stories were mine:
not the one where Mama fetched Clara a box
for bad-talking Grandma, nor the one where Icy
ran off to America to seek her fortune, and leave
Mama's good good brother to fend for himself.
Which he did. Ten years and three children later
Icy came back, shipped him out like parcel.

And always, as Aunty slid in the last pin
I'd cry "ouch", and she'd say,
"Now you pretty again."

COLD LEMONADE

I hope your travels have made you
long for home, before the chill of winter
dries your bones into a too fragile
but comfortable exile. Don't forget the vines
covering the verandah rails, the sunshine
peeping through, nor sea breeze carrying
a midday drizzle. Before you lose your way
to another love, remember the shade
on your favourite Sunday seat where
you imagined grown-up life,
and after a bicycle ride
you sipped a glass of Mama's
ice-cold lemonade. Mama is on
the verandah now, looking out,
counting spinning wheels.
A shiver escapes her,
before she calls "time".

NOSTALGIC DECEMBER

One week was all I had
to shut out noise and
let my hair go dread,
to enjoy kinks in this sinking city.
Untangling tomorrows or
fishing lines – never easy.
Here I breeze by memories
that stained my heart.
I enjoyed a shot of rum
in a half-lit piano bar, served with
pizza at 2.00 am. I liked wading
through water-soaked ground-
floors to discover intricately
sculpted marble statues –
"new experiences" promised,
no promises broken.
I laughed at myself, even
in the shivering cold, for being
a stick-in-the-mud kinda girl,
enthralled by Basilica di San Marco
and its ever-friendly residents,
speckled pigeons alighting
from every steeple to fly
between heaven and earth.
But bird shit soiled me – call it bad
luck to trip on an uneven step,
falling headlong into a fountain.
It was a blue hour to be happy,
to have sailed in a gondola, to
have sunlight overshadowing my past,
to cry out in your absence, amidst
the bright, colourful houses of Murano,
where the absence of noise would have
gone unnoticed.

EASTER SUNDAY MORNING

For Rex Nettleford

He found his feet
could not keep still
when Granny sing Sankeys
and brother Ben blow
the cow horn.

Granny watched him swaying,
skipping, kicking pupa lick,
turning back naysayers
with kongo drums,
fifes and sticks; nothing
could keep his feet from dancing.

So Easter Sunday mornings
we line up before sun up
in praise of Dinki Mini,
in praise of Kumina and Horsehead,
in praise of Pitchy Patchy
and Burru.
We learn that anticlockwise
spins, dips and breaks
connect to Glory.

SUNDAY VERANDAH STORY

Young-breasted girls tidy, wearing
short skirts and shorts; boys kotch
on the nearest verandah rail,
same as in our days.
Miss Maisie daughter pregnant,
Lue gone a foreign and Deacon suspicious.
A few young men riding bicycles,
girls braiding hair and Mas John
from the corner shop still blaring his new
music-set and selling rum too dear.
Madge, the town-happy girl, ready for anything...
But the board house change to concrete
and jade vines curling through
the lattice work replaced
by bright plastic flowers.

MAKING PLANS TO LEAVE

For years I wondered about leaving
my one hundred and forty four miles
island home.

I'm now certain mother planted
my navel string under rockstone
near my birthplace.

Tied, yes, I am tied to this land
like woman tie man with stew peas
so he must stay home.

Now I stand on the cliff face
in Oracabessa studying the open sea,
having overturned many stones.

Knowing a prophet is without honour
in his own country, I hear a sorry lost
weeping through sea sprays,

a hoarse chanting of my name
pulling out to sea, a rolling of waves,
and a salting of many waters echoing.

A dragonfly is busy overhead
trying to give me direction as I arrange
for dust and winding sheets to return.

MAMA SAID THERE WOULD BE DAYS LIKE THIS

When fireflies no longer
light the night sky, when the fluteman's
music dies down, band members
disperse, her poet friend caps
his pen for another season,
she lies wordless, struggling,
drawing laboured breaths. Mama said
there would be days of the unthinkable:
the swinging, twisting streets silenced;
the voices of her children fading; she
no longer able to dive into the Caribbean Sea;
East Indian mangoes no longer sweet.
Mama also said, tears or no tears,
La luta continua.

BROKEN BOTTLES

No one could explain the splintering sounds
that accompanied Mother's absence;
some say she went to offload
a mountain of emptiness into a nagging hollow.
She sought rest from stale liquor, had no choice but
to utter rivers of silence, no choice but to fly above
the children she was tending. The mender
of promises, our sanctuary, withdrew into
a quiet place, hoping that no one would notice.
But splintering bottles pierced the night;
the rattle of bottle on bottle, bone on bone
called us out as she emptied her throat.
An escape of sorts had her breaking
ties with old friends; splitting darkness
heaped in a backyard bottle mountain.
No comprehending her blank stare
nor her erratic movements. But time, the mender,
returned her in three weeks – as if she'd never left.
But we could never erase sharp images
and the fear of broken bottles.

SWEET MILK CREEK

That sort of town, that sort of love,
the names of places: Sweet Milk Creek
and Corn Valley, like flashes of happy
you showed me years ago. I quietly
board the train at Albany, have time to
study trees – bent, leafless,
split branches, even dead trees
exposing roots.

A crescent moon piercing twilight,
no innocence lost, no religion found,
only a clanging last mile. Pitch black
concrete boulders reveal themselves,
scaffolding-hoisting platforms signalling
a way out. The train pulls into a station.
For you I am here, bearing the weight
of winter, turning away from a life I no
longer care for; I tarry a while.

You are sound of light and corn
falling on my ear, shelling me out.
I am that man fishing on the Hudson
trusting his weight on thin ice, not angling
for cover, not worried about danger lurking.
An old sea-goer put out from port, confident
of the route traversed time and time again
through fog, high tide, tumultuous seas,
through countless winters.

A freighter hull marked by yellowing sides
makes straight the way, one more time,
the journey, watchful and deliberate
through sun-high days, moon-blotted
nights. We borrow beauty in measure

irrespective of the due date. We follow
the north star, hooked,
to an invisible finger.

TRAVELLING UNDER

My first time dancing counter-clockwise

was more of a trial run, an attempt to discover their secrets.
A great grand "Mother", dancing healing into baptisms, into wakes
on her mission ground, coloured flags waving away pain and heartbreak.

There was clapping, drumming, groaning and more clapping.

The dancing had my head spinning, feet hurting.
I was on to something: "Is time… is time, time to go
to Zion, time to fly."

With flowers, fruits, rum, and water on the table

it became clear, as turbaned heads danced round me
in rich regalia, in welcome, in groaning, as they
laboured for me, it became clear… the sky-spirit would enter.

Yashundi, Yashundai, cancan cada,
Yashundi, Yashundai, cancan cada.

DANCE, GIRL, DANCE

"Music, you can't stop it.
It took a long time to get
these ready-to-give-up legs
here. Play another nice one, girl."
She pulled her 89-year frame
onto the floor, and danced.
"You two don't know
the limbo walk or off-limit, eh?
Pity the swelling tek these legs;
can't show off again."
But for a while she did
shake off some distant verse.

READER WOMAN
For Tanya

Is you inspire me, girl.
You, who hang-up ballet shoes
by their wooden necks and kill
the tutu after it nearly kill you.

See, big bone *or kukumkum* bone,
it matters not. You find love
or maybe love find you. All it
tek was one reading

fe him to read you up,
know you is the girl God send
all the way from the West Indies,
to come stir foreign up.

How powerful is this word,
and him is number one reader,
no St. Thomas reader-man better. You
use tape measure, assess him and

nothing coming up short!
Him seh, him alone know when and where
to touch you, where and when to search
things out. Belief can kill and it can cure.

Is you inspire me, girl;
you don't know how long I looking for it,
teking me chance and writing it down,
that when my time come to get a read up

I will find one who know to read right,
not a pretend reader – for when and where
he lay his hands, must make everything rise.
You is a prophet girl. Speak the word.

SISTER BERNICE
(Passing the Kumina Baton, 2014)

Sister Bernice was a cousin, so we get it.
Giftings pass from mother to daughter, father to son.
Where there's no direct descendant, it pass to cousin,
like the throne of England.

Bernice Henry of Port Morant was the reigning
Kumina Queen. Not her fault she get it after Papa John
tek way himself before we born; he follow the river down
from Spring Hill to turn teacher, closing chapter.

But it was a haunting, this compulsion – I had to dance.
No surprise when the track John set before us,
book and bag schooling, take us back to great great granny
Mama Minott, the original Kumina queen.

Duty-bound I went to the send-off for Bernice, her feet
no longer responding to drum beats. I was spectator
till Jim raised *Roll Jordan Roll*. It was then the weeping
and jumping seize me. I joined the circle moving to Bandu

around the coffin: the wailing, the jumping, the twirling
was tribute to her tireless feet; as the spirit moved upon us,
Kumina baton was passing, as we sang *Roll Jordan Roll*,
as we roll on the ground. I wanted to claim it, wanted

to assure her that Kumina was safe, for Rex
who journeyed to Portland and baptize,
had in turn baptize many, not knowing that
one of the many was a rightful inheritor.

I touch her face in the coffin; it put on a shine,
same time they pick up on the chorus:
"Roll Jordan, roll. My soul arise in heaven Lord
Roll Jordan, roll."

SHABBA

Edit yourself, big man,
edit yourself. If you don't try
you discredit yourself.
Teacher tek chalk,
mek mark on my forehead,
den drop her word,
"Ready target for a bullet."
Teacher turn me out
on the streets:
"One or both will kill you."
But music big
bigger than death,
bigger than prison,
bigger than that.

I wear teacher's mark
like a magnet, every turn
I turn was a police dragnet.
But the music, it save me,
the music, it claim me.
No more dutty Babylon
for now I understand
that the music, it tame me.
It bigger than death
bigger than prison
bigger than that.

A real bad man
know when he is safe;
now I honour all deejays
who came before me.
Big Youth and Josie Wales
make me wear Clarks shoes,
Arrow shirt and terylene pants.

Never see it coming,
a way to dodge the bullets,
but the music big,
bigger than death
bigger than prison
bigger than that.

STRAW FLOWERS GROWING IN MIAMI LIKE WEED

I.

When my sister crossed over to you
I dreamt of bumblebees swarming.

She packed her two babies – boy and girl –
and flew across a "pearly everlasting" sky,

in a haze of smoke. My body sobbed,
not on the bed, not in the room. I followed

a curved sound-wave into a diorama.
Perhaps, bumblebees know nectar is sweet anywhere.

II.

In the dream only one man-size bee returned.
I watched him banging on my closed window,

his golden childlike fuzz seared, dripping red,
bulging "nigger-eye" acquired on his journey,

his crossover dragging me through timelessness
in a cartoon horror series. I cannot watch.

III.

A child's cry.
I watched him on his hallucinatory stage.
Kermit the frog and Oscar the grouch
would speak; he would answer;
no straight talk needed among pals.

Robbing the store was Kermit's plan.
They all went along. The police came.
He stood alone, hands bound. They stuffed him
into the squad car, like mother did
a dollar bill into her bag.

IV

On the inside
        there was no point of view,
his letters said,
        searching for a place without memory.
Every now and again
        Kermit or Oscar showed up;
there was no malice among friends,
        till the smoke cleared and they vanished.

ROMPING SHOP

(Every Man must have a Gal)

Buy your fantasies here!
Take me, spin me like a top,
and with each turn, each arch,
each needy caress, kill me, draw me
out, first giggling… Kill me again
before alighting like morning.

FIRE DEH A MUSS-MUSS TAIL

There is always a cool breeze
in the hills of Portland. Muss muss
don't know that breeze working
with Maroon – lure invaders into huts
then lull dem to sleep. Dem who search
for us glad to get inside a make-believe
fort – thatch-roof huts left vacant.
They march with muskets,
out-gunning our *buttas*.
They carry food and water,
while we, who are under science,
cannot risk smoke from fire,
live off berries and raw fish.
Early morning, after three,
when bakra fast asleep, we mek
poison *buttas*, and fire the thatch
from high up. In the trees
we watch the hut catch fire.
So dem come out, so we kill them.

NAVIGATING THE MIDDLE PASSAGE

I set aside the cube of Kabaa,
the aftershock of being erased,
choosing to believe in the network
of travelling tap roots and the mist from
the wide ocean, to tell stories
of lembe space, and field hollerers
limitless in building spirit bones
and tree tops; to fashion renewal
of river bottom and coral reef
with xplantation psyche
of praise. Praise and more praise
for Ashanti, Kikuyu, Mandingo, praise.
Praise and more praise for revival
gatherers, praise. Praise and more praise
for underwater currents travelling us up
to the utmost corners of the earth.
Praise.

NO SALT

Grandy Nanny was no Bongo.
Bongo talk and talk all de time
but Grandy Nanny sight the play:
no singing on the ship on the way
over, no answer no question.
She dumb herself, swallow the
obeah till she reach land,
then she shit it out. Grandy
Nanny fool dem; she eat no salt
so she could fly high, high above
the white blinding clouds. Bongo
never fly, only Maroon can fly.
So tomorrow morning
if you don't see me,
me gone.

ON THE EDGE OF THE WORLD

Poor Dorlene. She never know bush tea,
never sing calypso nor dance soca,
never know the delight of jumping
born naked into the river,
feel the cool water wash over and soothe
the hurts of Africa, her girlish pleats
locked tight. Too much passing of exams
not good for a girl; that's how Dorlene learn
to count the dead, save up newspaper
clippings, trip over her would-be lovers,
accepting talk 'bout nice men don't read.
But what Dorlene really want, she never
find in any book; when she start look
is when the other side bruck out.
No reclaiming Dorlene.

STICKFIGHTERS
(After reading *The Wine of Astonishment*)

Everybody want to be Bolo,
dancing again the sacred dance,
fire to fire; passions don't melt away
easy. Old people say,
Mark what a man leave behind.
But why my Caribbean scribe
should write we down so,
recording Yankee occupation
and how all we woman turn whore?
For if is so they think
about the spike heel,
red lipstick and tight skirt,
they can't see the stick
we wield to wage our war,
tek woman rhythm, mek song,
picking up a few lost
treasures here and there,
like secret soldiers covered
in seaweed, a camouflage
against ambush. But soon
we will gather again;
rain upon rain wash Bolo,
wash me, wash you.

KUMINA QUEEN

That my step is your step,
that the movement in me is not
one to keep, but to pass on,
that Bongo is a sweet word
although Mother used
it as a reprimand,
that when my bare feet
meet earth, the current
travelling uplifts me
and I forget the part of me
schooled in containment
and I dance the dance
of Ma Minott, skipping over
generations of pastors,
teachers, seamstresses
keeping me in, holding me back.
I must satisfy an ache coded
in the bloodline; in time
I must cross over the ocean
back to Zaire.

SOLD AGAIN (GENERATION NOW)

Old language can't reach me.
I'm one of the hip-hop, baggy pants
bling dog posse. To teach me
you got to understand
the vision in my grille,
understand why I've rejected the
the X and Y theories for this story.
They are building more jails,
rooms of no return,
where they put our mamas to lie
bellies to the ground.
They beat them then,
they beating us now.
That is why we dazzle
with diamond studs,
call our mamas whores,
our brothers dogs
and daddies nigger.
I ain't no clown,
just tripping till
the still-being-born
constitution is born.

SILENCING THE STONES

Nine-year-old girl pulled from the rubble
fifteen days after the earthquake,
hope for survivors gone.
Funeral fires lit, she stirred
among ghoulish companions,
her hair dressed in dust.
But when she opened her eyes
she rivalled the sun.

ADDICTION

My inner voice wants me
dead, wants me to make sense
of nonsense, wants to bleach me clean
as cocaine on a glass table top.
I search for you, bar hopping
and speed dating a sure hit – safe,
packaged and ready for pleasure.
I want free from too deep a fix.
I unwrap the package – myself –
like a present, a sacrament.
I hear the voice; I question.
"Who made you mine?" I sigh.
"No time but the present," you say.
"Let us together find wonder."
Against all logic, I taste, I swallow.
Death feels like sugar in my mouth.

GARDENER'S JUSTICE

Half sentences could not hide
the body of a ghetto youth:

"Him dead, ma'am… the funeral…
can't afford to feed myself.

Face down…
hot street, ma'am…

an we know the bwoy…
grow side a we.

Fred baptize in big church,
now Pastor no wa'an bury him."

He held the cutlass tight,
his hand shook.

"So they hold the killer yet?"
"No, ma'am, him still alive."

LYCHEE GUARD

As a little girl I avoided death notices.
It was as if by looking I would cause
someone close to be pulled.
Funny how things change.
Thirty years ago, girls walked
unmolested on the streets,
houses needed no steel bars,
laden lychee trees no guard.

DUPPY RUN

Early morning. Sunshine bounce back
off bottles dangling from the almond tree
in Mr Pink's yard, like spirit that won't rest.
"I swear to you, throwing salt on doorstep
not enough for today's advancements.
Tek more than that these days," Pink said.
"Left Jamaica as a boy." Now seventy-five,
his childhood worries linger. Looming
high in the almond tree, he set
protection fi ketch any bounce-back.
People say he returned home to get rid
of the cold clipping his bones,
or to better understand his need
to decorate almond tree like Christmas
all year round. Twenty-nine recycled plastic
bottles full of water, dangling. I guess
he discovered plastic progress in the First World,
moved ahead of us. Now, when he scream at night,
cowering in his bed, shaking like leaf,
is plastic he see, and not duppy.

BLOOD FLOWERS

(Tribute to Mary, mother of Jesus & mothers
who still carry the burden of slavery.)

I make myself know the child,
the one who survived the dark hold,
the sea-coffin burial, to inherit a land
of blood flowers.

He's in exile, his brother overboard,
his father lost. Only Mary, maybe Mary,
or maybe it was mother pounding
the blood-soaked earth.

The earth bloomed. Tall trees,
wrapped in the colour of death,
the restless Flame of the Forest,
walking with the lost, uphill.

A seed planted in the ground
multiplied. In sacrifices paid, I sing
hallelujah, hallelujah, hallelujah, for all
blood flowers in the fields are mine.

POINT OF VIEW

My garden holds no ambiguities.
My red gingers are red,
my allamandas startling yellow,
the grass an untroubled green;

yet my neighbour insists
there are mysteries
in my garden –
shapes without voices –

for he has been watching
the curves of the land
and the weeding,
and he can't understand

why my bending
and stretching upset him so.
He has become quite philosophical
about which end is up.

LAST RITES TO MENSES

I would have celebrated your passing,
if only I could pin down a date
like a menstrual cloth,
fold it neatly,
put it aside,
although forty years of sun
on the river stone
have left it a little ragged.
I'd want to celebrate
the work, the knowledge gained
when the river was steady:
how black pants hide stains
and running water reveals secrets.
If any of this mattered
I'd summon the sisters
to chant and clap –
if any of this mattered.
Forty years passed so quickly,
and two grown children later,
there is no certainty.
I missed you for a month or two,
no troubling show, no red dress.
Well, girl, bittersweet goodbye.

RIC

Ric stepped off the train in Manhattan,
said he stepped off the train before,
after Vietnam and two failed marriages,
after deaconizing and jail time.
Now Ric wakes up trembling
every time a train rattles
through his tunnel home.

Last time I saw him
he had started walking south
on the northbound line.

RIGHT TO DIE

I could not imagine
wanting Grandma dead;
having hurdled the years of
discontent and disagreement,
she was my compass at midnight.

There must be one such grandma
in every household, the one
who buried all our mournings
in her body while she ironed
and cooked breakfast; cracked
the surface of the earth with
mint plants she had placed gently
into the earth, to earn money
for the days when mother and
father came up short.

But the day of darkness came.
"Unfavourable," the surgeon said.
The feet of the river cut, all attempts
to bring laughter failed.
He was "duty bound to keep hope
alive". "Alive?" I searched his taut
expressionless face. Eyes fidgeting,
he flexed cramped fingers. "Enough,"
I said. A tear marked her pillow.

There would be no more tube feeding.
No more oxygen pumped in her lungs.
"Enough," I said. And as if she heard me
she sighed and took one last breath.

SIGN BIRDS
(You May Choose to Believe in Omens)

White owl flying early evening
across garden walls in the line of
sight; ivy trailing. Ivy had
come to say farewell, having left
worrisome leaves behind. Swaying
poinciana branches once helped
her upward climb. There she
had met starlings nesting in boles,
parakeets greening the evening sky,
and redheaded woodpeckers
drumming out a chorus. Now
the evening song was in her own
tongue: "Aileen, Carol,
Patricia, Marie and Len,
farewell."

DEAD CHILDREN ARE DEAD

(for Kehinde Wiley)

Growing up on the south side,
I had to hide from dogs, rat bats
and other dealers in the underworld.
They never held me; heaven knows
they tried. I was too busy tracking
Daddy over Nigerian hilltops, or
sketching Mama running for her
next bus, to get to her next job,
to pay the next rent – always late.
I'd paint the plane that would
lift us from the squalor, capture
the rise in uneven brush strokes
and my imagination, as vivid as
my travail. In a valley of mirrors
I was invisible. Nothing invisible
now in the High Museum of Art,
no leaving behind Mama's cruse of paint
overflowing. No telling the whole truth
of young men abandoned to the streets.
Dead children are dead: Mama's warning
left colours seeping out of me like blood.

DIRECT DEBIT

Direct debit, and so
his bills were paid,
house lights burning;
no one saw him
for the last five years
or missed him.

Only his skeleton was found
before the TV set
that had also burned out.

TRAVEL ADVISORY
(*Don't Go to the Park*)

Maybe I was overcome. I had to speak out!
I held an *Elm City Echo*, and asked, "Have you read this?"
The ten at the table shook their heads. "Only a dollar," I said.
I felt their pain coursing through me like life.

I had arrived just after the hotel kitchen closed at 10.00 p.m.
Having travelled five hours and twenty minutes
on a "chips only flight", I needed no reminder
of Maslow's hierarchy of need.

The concierge gave me a map, circled a point on Temple Street.
"A brisk ten minute walk, or you could call a cab," he said.
I decided to walk; after all this was a safe college town
and I was a traveller of sorts.

The bells were pealing, each inlaid stone reporting.
I wanted to touch, touch, and touch again stone walls,
not in the least bit troubled by graven images, subplots and motifs.
The imposing Christ Church offered sanctity enough,

the stained glass windows overshadowing intricate
mouldings, turrets, archways, woven as a woman would weave
a brocade fit for her only love, to be worn *in the season of fruitfulness*
when all things conspire together for good.

The wealthy do not know this; they hear bells,
see blossoms, but they who live in open spaces find the flowers
and the bees are irritants. Rain is a curse, and snow is death.
Many die each winter. "Take this cup Lord", I heard whispered.

I counted one, two, three, four, five, six, sitting
on park benches, as if they were out to enjoy the evening breeze.

I saw the seventh as he wrapped himself around an oak tree;
in the shadows he and the exposed root became one.

The eighth and the ninth could have been workmen pausing
on their way home, but *bag and pan* gave them away.
Then there was number ten. "Were not ten at the table?"
I heard a small voice ask. I looked up and saw the sky open;

a bird flew down and sat on the shoulder of a homeless man.
The man, accustomed to being buffeted, did not see, did not feel,
did not hear that the city had grown talons, and underground
chambers were now exposed in the park.

So when the sister took the *Elm City Echo*,
feeling my pain, she begged, "Don't Go To The Park."

WHITE ROSES

(for Norma who no longer buys white roses)

He gave her a dozen white roses.
From the first he'd acknowledged
his captivity to her free spirit,
but could not, or would not leave
his permanent arrangement.
Twenty years was something, after all,
and she had done all that a wife should do.
But Rosa was all that he longed for –
her laugh, her smile, her warmth,
her kiss. With her, all that
he desired bloomed, till love
gave way to memory.
Rosa withdrew her laughter,
closing in like a prayer leaf.
It was not knowing why
that bothered him. Why she sent
a dozen white roses
and a prayer card
before she hanged herself.

BIRD SHOOTING SEASON
(for Don Banks)

He died peacefully
just before bird-shooting season.
At the funeral
many birds flew by
the church doors.
One daring nightingale
fluttered restlessly
among the pews,
causing a stir. Some said
he'd come back as a bird,
but I believe
the birds had heard the news.
He'd been the best shot,
so they had sent
reconnoitring flights
to be sure that this giant
was not just ailing
but put down for good.

DROP-PAN GAME

If your surname's Campbell, there's a fifty-fifty chance
you'll catch ninety. As I never fail to remind
Chicky, "Girl, look at us now, can barely crawl;
all our friends play three. I tell death,
tek a chance. But death don't hear me,
pass me over. Death is like a man
stalking girl he can't afford.
But half a luck is chance,
and every now and again
the number you pick will play,
so pick a number, Chicky,
pick a number, and pray."

2008 NEWS REPORT ON FIDEL
(for Dewey)

Death wrestled the giant
and won,
silenced the revolution.
Anti-Fidel celebrants
gathered,
but, at home, the liberator
listened
to the radio broadcast
and smiled once more.

CASKET PIECE

Mek and put down some twenty years,
Maas Ralph well prepare; after all
not everything set up like rain.
Granny, who grow him, live higher up
the mountain (could almost hear
celestial trumpet sounds),
teach him: "Don't invite strangers
home in case the smaddy
turn out to be unwelcome
an you can't turn them back."

Death must be like the trek to Ralph's
house — thorny, steep —
a journey to think twice about.
The dense overgrowth keeps
casual visitors out. Maas Ralph had
long ago chopped the wood for his
final box, resting on top
the cupboard in the kitchen. He said
"I mek my peace with God
long time."

FINAL OFFICE

Dear Esteemed Life,
I hope you will use your good offices to see me through.
I've contemplated the goings-on here
and find that lingering is in poor taste.
Over the years I've amassed a mountain
of paper, elastic bands, and paper clips –
too much for office scissors to cut through –
so I write formally to request help. Knowing
that you are duty bound, I am expecting a
stuffer or shredder. Someone mentioned that
the final office will be cold and welcoming
and a name tag is affixed to newcomers
for easy identification.

Working it through,
Ignota

ABOUT THE AUTHOR

Monica Minott is a chartered accountant. She has received two awards in the Jamaican National Book Development Council's annual literary competitions for book-length collections of her poetry. She was awarded first prize in the inaugural Small Axe poetry competition. Her poems have been published in *The Caribbean Writer*, *Small Axe Caribbean Journal*, *Cultural Voice Magazine*, *SX Salon*, *Jubilation*, *Coming Up Hot* and *The Squaw Valley Review*, and more recently in *BIM* magazine. Some of her poems have been broadcast on Power 106 in Jamaica.